Our Father

Public Prayers
for All Occasions

by J. Michael Shannon

STANDARD
PUBLISHING
Cincinnati, Ohio

To my daughter, Angela,
who is herself
an answer to many prayers,
but especially mine

Library of Congress Cataloging-in-Publication Data
Shannon, J. Michael.
   Our Father : public prayers for all occasions / J. Michael
   Shannon.
       p. cm.
   ISBN 0-7847-0398-1
   1. Prayers. 2. Pastoral prayers. I. Title
BV245.S47   1995
264' . 13–dc20   95-13615
                                                  CIP

The Standard Publishing Company, Cincinnati, Ohio
A division of Standex International Corporation
©1995 by The Standard Publishing Company
All rights reserved
Printed in the United States of America

02 01 00 99 98 97 96 95   5 4 3 2 1

CONTENTS

Introduction 5
Baptism Prayers 9
Benedictions 11
   Biblical Benedictions 12
Church Business/Events
   Athletic 13
   Baby Day..14
   Board Meeting...15
   Church Supper...16
   Congregational Meeting............................17
   Dedication of Building..............................18
   Groundbreaking...19
   Missions...20
   Ordinations 21
   Revival...23
   Travel 24
   Wedding 25
Civic Prayers 26
Communion Prayers 28
Funeral Prayers 31
   Accident 33
   Aged 34
   Child 35
   Graveside 36
   Long Illness 37
   Murder 38
   Suicide...39
   Teenager..40

Prayers for Health
    Hospital Patient..41
    Newborn...42
    Nursing Home...43
    Recovery...44
    Shut-Ins...45
    Surgery...46
    Terminally Ill...47
Invocations 48
    Biblical Invocations.....................................52
Offering Prayers 54
Pastoral Prayers 60
    Biblical Pastoral 85
Seasonal Prayers
    New Year..92
    Youth Sunday 93
    Good Friday...94
    Easter 95
    Mother's Day...98
    Memorial Day..99
    Pentecost...100
    Graduation 101
    Father's Day...102
    Independence Day 103
    Thanksgiving...104
    Christmas...107
Time of Tragedy 111

INTRODUCTION

When I was a young minister, a member of my congregation told me, "Don't call on me to pray in public; I don't believe in it. Jesus said we should pray in our closet."

I didn't have a good answer then, but I do now. Jesus practiced public prayer. For instance, He prayed over the Lord's Supper when He instituted it. What about the model prayer that we call the Lord's Prayer? How would we even know the Lord's Prayer if He had not offered it publicly? As with many aspects of worship, there are public and private components to prayer. Yes, there are times when prayer is intensely private. Still, there are other times when the minister or some other worship leader is asked to word a prayer on behalf of the corporate body of Christ. This is a great challenge often neglected. Formal churches read beautiful prayers from prayer books, yet there is so much repetition that the words become like background music in an elevator. People in less formal churches offer spontaneous prayers, but they end up sounding the same note week after week.

The purpose of this book is to give those who offer public prayers some ideas to stimulate their thinking and give them a resource for Sunday and beyond. Some people believe there is something wrong with planning prayers before they are prayed. While a spontaneous prayer has its place, must all conversations be spontaneous? Even in our personal conversations, if our cause is important enough and we want to be clearly understood, we think out our words before we speak them. The planning does not negate the sincerity of the thought. It is the author's hope that this humble contribution will ignite a new appreciation for the prayers of worship.

The purpose of this modest volume is to give you suggestions and models for your public prayers. This would include both prayers offered in public worship, but also prayers that would be offered publicly in other aspects of church ministry, such as prayers for weddings, funerals, baptisms, hospital calling, and countless other occasions.

One of the goals of this book is to provide

dignified but contemporary prayers. This means that the vocabulary used will be the vocabulary of the average worshiper. It is good to remember that the words "Thee" and "Thou" were not originally special prayer words. There was a time when these words were used in the informal circle. It is we who have assumed that "Thee" and "Thou" is "church talk." For this reason these words will not be used in these prayers.

Some counsel as to the principles of public prayer might be in order. First, remember you are not just representing yourself, but also the community of believers. You are trying to put into words what the worshipers would say if they could. Second, you preachers may want to give as much attention to your prayers as to your sermons. Actually, a case could be made that you might want to give more attention to the prayers. After all, in a prayer you are talking to God. Third, avoid flowery language. This does not mean that our prayers should be stilted and prosaic. It does mean that excessive description and ostentatious language no longer reflects the way we communicate today.

Finally, don't be afraid to be brief. We can remember, or at least have heard, stories about prayers that lasted longer than sermons. These kinds of prayers rarely speak for the congregation. To recommend brevity is not to diminish the importance of prayer, but it is important to remember that the average worshiper's attention span has shrunk considerably. Just as sermons and other public messages tend to be shorter, so too should be our prayers. God, of course, will be listening, but the audience will not and we are supposed to be speaking for them. Even in a simpler, more forgiving time, Jesus counseled that prayers are not to be judged by their length. Even then, vain repetition was declared to be sin. We will always feel, to some extent, that our prayers are inadequate. It is that divine dissatisfaction that keeps us praying. Our request is ever the same as disciples of old who asked Jesus, "Lord, teach us to pray."

Dear Lord, what a marvelous picture we see today. When we see this ordinance we think back to the cross. As Jesus took our place on the cross, so we take His place in this passion play of grace. Help us also to look at our own lives. We want to put our old selves into the grave and rise to live the resurrected life with Your Son. Bless the one(s) who submit(s) to Your ordinance today, but may we all find our faith strengthened as again we see life born of death. We pray in the name of Jesus, whose death give meaning to what we see today, amen.

BAPTISM

Almighty God, who receives those who come for mercy, we call upon You on behalf of Your servant who comes to the waters of baptism even as You have commanded. We come in faith and in an attitude of repentance, knowing that this moment is the fulfillment of Your covenant with us. In this moment we can see a death to sin. In this moment we see a resurrection to new life. In this moment we see a cleansing. Because of the Christ of the cross, we pray. Amen.

And now to the Father, the one who will never forget us, to the Son, the one who intercedes for us, and to the Spirit, the one who dwells within us, be everlasting glory and honor and praise both now and forever. Amen.

Now may the Father be your only God, may the Son be your only guide, and may the Spirit be your comfort, this day and every day. Amen.

Now may the Lord grant us His peace, even though our hearts are troubled. May He grant redemption, even though we are undeserving. May He grant us great opportunities, even though we are flawed. We pray through Christ who makes it all possible, amen.

BIBLICAL BENEDICTIONS

The Lord bless you and keep you; the
Lord make his face shine upon you and be
gracious to you; the Lord turn his face
toward you and give you peace.

Numbers 6:24-26

Now to him who is able to do im-
measurably more than all we ask or
imagine, according to his power that is
at work within us, to him be glory in the
church and in Christ Jesus throughout
all generations, for ever and ever! Amen.

Ephesians 3:20

To him who is able to keep you from
falling and to present you before his glorious presence without fault and with great
joy—to the only God our Savior be glory,
majesty, power and authority, through
Jesus Christ our Lord, before all ages, now
and forevermore! Amen.

Jude 24, 25

We thank You, dear God, for the opportunity for friendly competition. We thank You for the benefits of physical activity in the body. We thank You for the lessons learned in athletic competition, lessons on teamwork, perseverance, and discipline. We thank You for the enjoyment we receive in the participation and observation of these events. We pray that those participating will display sportsmanship and a Christlike spirit. Keep these teams free from injury. Above all, help us to remember that this is a game. In Jesus' name, amen.

BABY DAY

Gracious God, we thank You for what children bring into our lives. They remind us of new hope and new possibilities. They also remind us of our responsibility to leave a legacy of faith to the next generation. Bless these children, that they may grow in the nurture and admonition of the Lord. As they grow, we pray that our example might draw them to Jesus. May we place no impediment in their way. In the name of Jesus, who always had time for the children, amen.

Lord, help us in this meeting to put aside our own agendas and align ourselves with Yours. Give us wisdom, for the matters before us are complex. Give us a spirit of calm, because the matters before us are sometimes controversial. Give us a spirit of unity for there is always the tendency to choose sides. We don't ask that we always agree, for differences of opinion are often the material used to build sound decisions. We do ask that we remain in the Spirit of Christ, in whose name we pray. Amen.

CHURCH SUPPER

Help us, dear God, to see the holiness of fellowship. It is in moments like these that we grow closer to each other. As we break bread together, we remember how Jesus shared the table with His disciples. We recall how in His resurrection He fixed breakfast for His followers. Grant that our bodies will be renewed by the food, even as our spirits are renewed by the fellowship. Thank You for the loving hands that have done great service through the preparation of this meal. We would ask that Your Spirit be among us so that He may be our special guest. In the dear name of Jesus we pray. Amen.

We come together in this hour to consider the matters close to Your heart, O God, and crucial to the health and vitality of Your church. Help us to cease all debate over who controls this church. It is not the minister, officers, or even the congregation that is preeminent. This church belongs to You. Help us to make every decision with that great truth clearly in view. Grant us wisdom and civility. We thank You for making us partners in Your great work. Through Christ who is the head of the body, amen.

DEDICATION OF A BUILDING

Father, we recognize that these walls are not a church, only a place to house the church. Nevertheless, a building is a great tool for the work of Your church. We offer this building to You as a place of worship, teaching, fellowship, and service. We trust it will be a beacon to our community. While we don't exalt the stones, we do exalt You and ask You to use this building even as You use us, the living stones. In the name of Jesus, the chief cornerstone, we pray. Amen.

Thank You, God, for new beginnings. Help us to complete the work You have called us to do. This ground is not holy because we will be placing a building here. It is holy ground because it is dedicated to Your service. Even as this ground is broken to make it useful, break our hearts, that You may build in our lives spiritual graces. In the name of Jesus the carpenter, amen.

MISSIONS

Loving God, we want You to bless the labors of our missionaries. We honor the sacrifices they have made. We pledge to support them with our funds, but even more with our prayers. Pick them up when they are discouraged. Relieve their loneliness by helping them feel a closeness to us as we pray, and to You as You bless. We know that all people of all nations were made in Your image. All have need of Your grace, and we thank You for those who are willing to make extraordinary efforts to bring Your Word to those who are far off. We pray for open doors. We pray that the kingdoms of this world will become of the kingdom of our Lord and Christ, where He shall reign forever. Amen.

Father, today we set apart this child of yours to become a servant of the church. This service is leadership. There is no greater calling than to be called to the ministry of the Word. It is a rare privilege and an awesome responsibility. Today we ask You to protect Your servant from the temptations that will surely buffet. We ask for Your protection from the discouragement that is inevitable in this mighty work. Grant to Your servant a keen mind to understand Your Word as well as the strategies that will enhance its impact. Grant to Your servant a warm heart to hurt with those who are hurting and to weep with those who are weeping. May none of us ever see this as just another job. We pledge ourselves to support and pray for those who labor in this special way. May Your Spirit be ever present in those who minster throughout the life of the church. We pray through Jesus, the object and subject of our preaching. Amen.

ORDINATION OF LEADERS

We set apart these servants, dear God, to become leaders in Your church. They take on a thankless task. They work without pay and will no doubt face criticism and disappointment. We pledge our support. Help us not to criticize but to affirm. Help us to build up, not tear down. Give Your servants wisdom, and protect them from the assaults of the evil one. Through the Lord, whose plan for changing this world was to work through people, amen.

Father, our prayer is simple; bring us revival. We know the revival tarries, not because the world does not act like Christians, but because Christians don't act like Christians. We know that revival will not begin when we point the finger at our neighbor. It begins when we look at ourselves and say, "God be merciful to me, a sinner." Revival is not just a mustering of enthusiasm, it is a surrender of life itself. Change us dear God, that we might change the world. Amen.

TRAVEL OF A CHURCH GROUP

Father, we commit this journey to You. Please be a companion to our brothers and sisters as they embark under the banner of our congregation. We know that nothing in this life is free from all risk. Still, we ask that You would spread a blanket of protection over our travelers. Keep them safe from the perils that sometimes afflict those away from home. Let this journey be to Your glory. Amen.

Gracious Father, author of love and life itself, we come today to celebrate the beautiful institution of marriage. We thank You that You gave this gift for the nurture and support of Your children. Even in the midst of celebration, we acknowledge the need of Your strengthening presence. Those whom we unite in marriage today will treasure many joys, but they will also endure many hardships. Give them grace to face each challenge with confidence and assurance. Help them to grow in mutual love and affection. May each challenge only draw them closer to each other and to You, the source of their strength. Help them to see that it takes only a moment to commence a marriage, but it takes a lifetime to create a marriage. We pray through Christ, who brought joy to a wedding feast in Cana. Amen.

A CIVIC OR SERVICE CLUB

Almighty God, we thank You for the opportunity to serve. We recognize our need to serve You and our community. We would be impoverished if we had not accepted the service others have rendered in our lives. We wish to honor them and You by dedicating ourselves to healing the brokenhearted, to uplifting the downcast, to caring for less fortunate. Fulfill our hope to bring a ray of light into the lives of those who are surrounded by the darkness of despair. Help us to make our community, nation, and world a better place because of our service. Grant us success in these matters, but not for our own glory. We ask these things through Him who loved us and gave himself for us, amen.

Dear Lord, we acknowledge that You designed human government, and Your Scriptures teach us to respect the rule of law. We ask today that You would send Your blessings to these who seek to serve through leadership in government. Grant them wisdom, for the issues are complex. Grant them courage, for the decisions are often unpopular. Give them a heart for this work that puts the public good over personal gain. We pray in the name of Him who taught us that the way to real leadership is through service, and that the way to true honor is through sacrifice. Amen.

COMMUNION

This is Your table, Lord, and we can claim no right to be here. We come at Your invitation. We don't deserve to be here apart from the sacrifice of the Lord Jesus who made us Your children. The nails should have been ours. The crown of thorns should have pierced our brows. The cross should have been our destiny. We are weak, O Lord, and like those disciples of old, we have betrayed, denied, and deserted Christ Jesus. Even so, You welcome us here and treat us as honored guests. We can't appeal to our record, but we gratefully appeal to Your loving heart. In spite of all the evidence to the contrary, You know that we love You. Even though we don't deserve it, we will accept Your invitation and enjoy the benefits of this feast. Who are we to decline Your invitation? Though we will never be worthy, we do pray that our lives will display our respect for You and Your Son. In His precious name we pray. Amen.

Father, we accept the invitation of Your Son to join You at this table. Though these elements are common, they are made uncommon by Your Son. His sacrifice for us has forever sanctified the bread and the cup. We take this bread and it becomes for us the body of the Lord Jesus, reminding us that He gave of himself completely. We take this cup and it becomes for us the blood of the Lord Jesus, who shed His own blood for our sins.

As we take in these elements, help us to see that we must internalize for ourselves the blessings of the cross of Christ. In His dear name we pray. Amen.

COMMUNION

We treat this time, dear Father, as a feast. Though we eat just a bit of bread, and drink just a small portion of juice, this is a feast because it fills us and nourishes us spiritually. These are common elements, but we can never look at them without thinking of how Jesus has forever transformed them. We look at this bread and see the body of Jesus. We look at this cup and see His shed blood. In these emblems we see the remission of our sins. We thank You for this memorial that will stand longer than any human effort. Long after memorials of stone crumble, Your church will gather around this table to remember Jesus. Long after tributes on paper have disintegrated, Your church will be celebrating this living, eternal memorial. We are grateful to be a part of this tradition. We are happy to obey the command of Jesus to remember Him. May Your Spirit be among us, drawing us to Christ, in whose name we pray. Amen.

Dear Father, we thank You that we don't have to face this dark day alone. We thank You for the presence of dear friends and family, but even more we thank You for Your presence. There is much pain in our hearts and many questions in our minds. We thank You that You are big enough to bear the pain and confusion with us. Help us to see that we are never forsaken. As we face a prospect of days ahead without the earthly presence of one we love, give us the grace to take life one day at a time. Since we know You are with us, we can face the prospect of moving on in our lives, even though we are burdened by grief. We don't understand why there must be death, but we know that Your Son experienced it also. As You showed us in Your Son, help us to see that death is not the final word. You have saved the last word for yourself and that word is "life." In the name of Him who said, "I am the resurrection and the life," we pray. Amen.

FUNERAL

Dear God, we know You are the author
of life. Even in this moment we ask You to
help us see life and not death, to see beginnings and not endings, to see hope and
not despair, to see faith and not doubt.
We know that You never promised that we
could avoid the valley of the shadow of
death, but You did promise to be there with
us. Anything that draws us closer to You
cannot be bad. Sanctify the memories we
have of our beloved. Take away the pain
of remembering. We mourn mostly for
ourselves because we cannot comprehend
life without the ones who have touched it
thus far. Fill the empty places in our lives
and let Your presence compensate us for
the loss. Dry our tears even as we look
forward to that place You have prepared,
where there will be no need for tears,
except perhaps the tears of joy and glad
reunion. Through Jesus, who through His
own death opened up the possibilities of
eternal life, amen.

THOSE WHO DIED IN AN ACCIDENT

We are dismayed this day, O God, by how suddenly calamity can come into our lives. In the midst of our shock and surprise, we ask You to heal the wounds in our hearts. Your Word promises us that You notice, even when the sparrow falls. We know that Your Word does not promise that we will avoid death, but that You will walk through the valley with us when the time is ours. Thank You for allowing us to lean on You. Amen.

ONE WHO DIED OF OLD AGE

Father, today we would honor a life well lived. Though our beloved has seen may days, nevertheless we are sad for our loss. We would not be selfish enough to call our beloved back for our own needs. We know that You provide a new body and a fellow-ship even greater than we enjoy here. We thank You for the wisdom age offers. May we take that wisdom and so live our lives that we might be worthy of the legacy we honor today. We pray in the name of Jesus who brings new life, amen.

O God, our throats are so choked with emotion that we can barely speak. Our minds are so full of questions that we can barely think. We even have a touch of anger, Lord. In the midst of this tragic moment, we ask that You would help us to feel Your warm embrace. Father, You taught us Your love for children. Even in eternity we ask that You would give special blessings to the little ones. We think today of pleasures that will not be enjoyed, but help us also to think of pains that will not be endured. This child will never lose the purity of innocence. This moment reveals to us the mingled joy and sorrow that accompanies love. Take our burden, for it is too heavy to bear alone. In the name of Christ, our Lord, amen.

GRAVESIDE SERVICE

Father, we can't help but be sad as we look over this solemn place. It is a place of beauty, but it is also a place of death. We recognize that our loved ones are not here and never were. Only the body their living spirit dwelt in lies here. Nevertheless, we cannot think of our loved ones apart from the body. So, sanctify this place for us, to be a place of remembrance. May we come to this quiet spot and remember those who have gone on before us.

Help us to say good-bye, even though it is difficult. We do not believe that this good-bye is final. Help us to believe that because Jesus conquered the grave, so will we. In the power of His resurrection we pray, amen.

Father, we give You thanks for eternal rest and peace. We have prayed so long for healing and now we accept that You have chosen to deliver healing through that new body in the eternal realm. We do not understand why some have to suffer for so long, yet we know that, as in the case of Your servant, Job, it is not a sign that You are angry with us. While we mourn the days of pain, we now celebrate the release of all earthly afflictions. We remember what your servant Paul has told us, that, "our present sufferings are not worth comparing with the glory that will be revealed in us." In the name of our living Savior, who suffered for us, amen.

A MURDER VICTIM

Father, today we face sorrow and anger— sorrow for our loss, and anger because of the injustice. It is hard for us to believe that evil so consumes a person that he chooses to take away Your precious gift of life. Even though our anger is justified, we ask that You would do a mighty work on the perpetrator of this horrid act. Bring this criminal to justice, but also to Your throne of grace. If through this tragedy some life can be brought from darkness to light, then this tragedy will be transformed into triumph. We pray in the name of Jesus, whose death at the hands of wicked men brought grace to all who will receive it. Amen.

Our minds are full of questions, Lord, questions that may never be answered in this life. We ask, "Why?" We wonder if there was anything we could have done. Relieve us from the storm of guilt and anger that swirls around us. Help us today to have compassion for our loved one. We may never be able to understand the inner pain and anger that led to hopelessness. So, help us to forgive. Help us to turn to You should such despair ever confront us. We are grateful that You understand our pain. You are mindful of our condition. Grant grace and peace this day. In the name of Jesus, who understands far better than we, amen.

FUNERAL OF A TEENAGER

Father, we are almost always surprised by
death. It seems to come too soon. Today
we feel this surprise even more acutely.
Help us to remember that life is not mea-
sured by how many years were in the life,
but how much life was in the years. We
pledge to remember, though remembering
is painful. Turn the bitterness of our
despair into sweet memories of the joyful
wonder and exuberance of childhood and
the days of youth. Let us not think so
much of missed opportunities, but rather
of the storehouse of memories we have to
enjoy. Let not the thought of the days we
wish we had make dark the beauty of the
days we did have. In the name of Jesus,
who also died young, amen.

Father, this very room can be a sacred place if You are here, so we ask for Your presence. While we do not enjoy this hospital stay, we do look forward to the blessing that can be ours as we turn to You in this time of stress. We call on You as the great physician to restore health to the body. We call on You as the encourager to lift our spirits. We call on You, our loving Father, to keep us ever ready for that life in which there will be no pain or sickness. We thank You for the doctors, nurses, and technicians who minister to our physical needs. Guide them and give them wisdom. Bless them in their labors. We ask that You bring that extra measure of healing that only You can supply. We pray through Christ who touched the sick and made them whole, amen.

A NEWBORN

We thank You, dear Father, for the safe delivery of this new life. Even in this joyous hour we are mindful of the dangers ahead. Please look with benevolence upon this new child. Help us to be the protectors and nurturers we need to be. Even as this child rests in the arms of parental love, may Your love become a living reality. Every new child is not only a precious gift to the family, but also a precious gift to the church and to the world. Help us to honor this gift. In the name of the One who came to us as a baby, amen.

Father, the days are long and often lonely. May this place be not so much an institution, but a home. We pray for good health so that each day may be an opportunity to experience the joy of living. We pray for rich fellowship so that each day may be filled with the blessings of friendship. We pray also for those who labor here. Encourage them as they encourage others. Meet their needs as they care for the basic needs of others. Let them know that their service is to Christ, in whose name we pray. Amen.

TIME OF RECOVERY

We thank You, dear Father, for delivering Your servant from bodily illness. We pray now that Your servant may devote this renewed strength to more vigorous service in Your kingdom. May the spirit be strengthened even as the body. We thank You for the progress that is evident. We pray for even more progress in the days to come. In the name of our blessed Redeemer, amen.

Father, we confess frustration today, the frustration of not having freedom to move, drive, and visit others. Father, so much time is spent imprisoned by inactivity. Let this be a time of spiritual renewal. Make this room not a prison, but a chapel where You will be worshiped. If we see Your Son's presence, then there is no loneliness.

Although Your servant may be limited physically, there is no limitation on his/her spiritual strength. Produce in this room a prayer warrior. This is indeed significant service. Let this room be a house of prayer.

In the name of our Friend and Companion, amen.

SURGERY

God, You know the fear that grips our hearts. You know that we face surgery with a sense of foreboding. We pray that You would guard, guide, and lead everything that happens in this upcoming surgery. We ask You to bless the doctors, nurses, and technicians who have devoted their lives to the healing of the body. We also ask that You would bring that extra measure of healing that only You can bring. Speed the time of recovery and bring freedom from pain. In the name of the great physician, amen.

Father, we come to You in the face of the most difficult news we can hear on this earth. We have heard the word "terminal," and we need to take that seriously. But, we do know, Father, that these matters are ultimately in Your hands. We ask You for restored health, healing, and the extension of life. If that is not what is to be, then we ask for comfort, peace, and freedom from pain. Even though the outward body may grow weak and sickly, we know You can provide inner strength, health, and beauty. None of us knows the number of our days, so help us to make each day count. Help us to see each day as a gift. May we fill each day with joy, love, and accomplishment. Through Christ, who is the author of hope, amen.

INVOCATION

Father, it has been a long week. We have faced problems and challenges of many kinds. There were times this week when we just wanted the day to be over. As we face this day, we don't know whether to cry over the problems of the past week, or smile at the possibilities of the new week. Make this service today a winnowing process. Remove that which is negative and leave behind that which is holy. May this service change us. In the name of Jesus we pray, amen.

Come among us, God of life. You have
given us physical life as well as eternal
spiritual life in Christ. Grant us now abundant life for this week. Accept our praise,
for it is from sincere hearts. We lift our
voices in prayer and singing. We desire
to worship You in Spirit and in truth.
Through Jesus, who is the way, the truth,
and the life, amen.

INVOCATION

Lord, we are ready. We are ready to see You. We are ready to serve You. We are ready to listen to You speak to us. This service is to acknowledge You and to praise You, and we marvel that even in this moment reserved for Your glory, You have been kind enough to meet our deepest needs. Through Your Son, who was the embodiment of Your presence, we pray. Amen.

We don't so much ask You to come among us, dear Father, as much as we ask You to make us conscious of Your presence. We know Your promise to be in our midst. While we know You are with us each day, You come to us in a special way when we gather together in Your name. May the offering of praise today be acceptable to You. May You be as real to us as the neighbor we stand beside. May we see You in the songs, prayers, ordinances, and the preaching of the Word. In Christ our Savior we pray, amen.

BIBLICAL INVOCATIONS

The Lord is in his holy temple; let all the earth be silent before him.

Habakkuk 2:20

Glorify the Lord with me; let us exalt his name together.

Psalm 34:3

I will exalt you, my God the king; I will praise your name for ever and ever. Every day I will praise you and extol your name for ever and ever. Great is the Lord and most worthy of praise; his greatness no one can fathom.

Psalm 145: 1-3

The Lord is my light and my salvation—whom shall I fear? The Lord is the stronghold of my life—of whom shall I be afraid?

Psalm 27:1

He who dwells in the shelter of the Most High will rest in the shadow of the Almighty. I will say of the Lord, "He is my refuge and my fortress, my God, in whom I trust."

Psalm 91:l, 2

Praise the Lord.
Praise God in his sanctuary;
   praise him in his mighty heavens.
Praise him for his acts of power;
   praise him for his surpassing greatness.
Praise him with the sounding of the
   trumpet,
praise him with the harp and the lyre,
praise him with tambourine and dancing,
praise him with the strings and flute,
praise him with the clash of cymbals,
praise him with resounding cymbals.
Let everything that has breath praise
   the Lord.
Praise the Lord.

Psalm 150

OFFERING

Help us, dear Father, to see the power of our gifts. So often we think that our little gift doesn't matter much. But our accumulated gifts—like a collection of raindrops—can become a powerful torrent. Help us to see that it is not the size of our gifts that You measure, but the size of our hearts. You can take our small gifts and multiply them as You did when one boy's lunch fed more than five thousand people. We pray that You will bless this offering. In the name of Him who noticed the widow's mite, amen.

Dear God, You have filled our lives with Your gifts immeasurable and un-fathomable. There are the gifts of friend-ship, family, church, and even the gift of life itself. We cannot give You anything that comes close to the gifts You have given us. Our need to give is far greater than Your need to receive. Nevertheless, we give our money, time, and talent because we desire to worship You. In the end, all we have to give is ourselves, but in the end that's all You ask. In the strong name of Jesus, amen.

OFFERING

We are staggered, dear Father, at the great needs present in this world. There are so many people who need basic necessities, and so many missions that need financial support. Help us to give freely out of our abundance. We have so much compared with the rest of the world. Father, relieve us from the desire to be rich and help us see that compared with most people on this planet, we already are. In the name of the greatest giver, our Lord Jesus, amen.

Dear God, we can give You nothing that is not already Yours. Still, You accept our gifts with a smile. You are the giver of every good and perfect gift, and if we are to be like You, we must give too. Out of loving hearts we bring our offerings, pieces of paper and metal that represent the labors of our lives. We want to support Your kingdom's work. Please accept these gifts and multiply them as they do good in the work of this church and through missions around the world. In the name of Jesus, who gives us love that becomes generosity, amen.

OFFERING

Lord, we are almost embarrassed to approach You with our gifts. You have given us so much, our gifts seem paltry in comparison. We offer these gifts with loving hearts, remembering that You notice the size of our hearts, not the size of our gifts. We give, not so much because the church has a need of gifts, but because we have a need to give. Please bless those entrusted with the proper distribution of these funds. Magnify our gifts beyond our ability to comprehend. Through Christ, the greatest gift of all, amen.

God, grant us the joy of giving. May we never see the opportunity to give as a burden, but rather a blessing. Bless those works, causes, and persons who will receive these offerings. In addition to the financial support, grant them a special power to do Your work. We pray through the Lord Jesus, who told us You love cheerful givers. Amen.

PASTORAL

Dear God, be our teacher this day. Teach us how to walk in the narrow way. Teach us how to say no to the things of this world. Teach us how to be more like Christ. Teach us how to love each other.

We confess that learning and growing is often painful. We have tried our own ways and found them wanting. Help us to see that growing in Christ is a lifelong process in which divine discontentment prompts us. Help us to proceed past the pain to find new vistas of Your love and grace. We submit to Your instruction. Teach us so that we may teach others Your ways. Through Jesus who was and ever remains our rabbi, amen.

Father, we are often foolish enough to believe that no one has suffered as much as we have, no one is as lonely as we are, and no one really understands. On this day we see the vanity of such thoughts. On this day we recognize that Jesus traveled a lonesome road. Jesus faced suffering that He did not deserve. Jesus endured ridicule and a violent death. These facts are sad enough, but sadder still when we consider that our sin put Jesus through all of this. Surely He has borne our sins and our sorrows. He died for sins that were not His own that we might have a righteousness that is not our own. May His cross find a place in our hearts to stand as a constant reminder that You love us, You are with us, You understand, and have provided life eternal. The cross is where we first saw the light. The cross is where forgiveness was made real. In the name of Jesus, who for the joy set before Him gave up His life, amen.

PASTORAL

Bind us together, dear Father. Bring us
to perfect unity with each other, even as we
are in perfect unity with Christ. We confess the sins that have brought disunity
and dishonor to Your name. Let the unity
we share be a testimony to a warring world
of the grace and mercy of the Lord Jesus.
Many are the forces and factors that would
seek to splinter us. Many are the harmful
things accomplished by our divisive spirit.
A united church, delivering a united testimony, would be a mighty force in this
world. Too often we see each other as the
enemy. Even the lost are not our enemy,
only victims of the enemy. While the
pressure of disunity is great, greater is the
One who binds us together. In His name
we pray. Amen.

Dear God, we surrender. It is an unconditional surrender. We give You free reign over our lives. We have struggled long enough trying to make our own plans work. We have suffered enough at the hands of our own agendas. We surrender our wills that we might obey, our bodies that we might glorify and serve, and our minds that we might apply wisdom to the problems of this world. In the name of Him who truly deserves to be called Lord, amen.

PASTORAL

Father, we plead today for Your divine
forgetfulness. We beseech You to remember our sins no more. All we have been
able to do is think about them constantly.
They haunt us and taunt us. They beat
down upon us and wear us down. Though
we have sinned, we do want with all our
hearts to please You. The spirit is willing,
but the flesh is weak. Grant us pardon for
sins past and give us power to overcome
temptations present. Give us the wisdom
to minister to others in compassion. Help
us to relieve suffering rather than to cause
it. Help us to build up rather than to tear
down. Help us to be concerned, not so
much with our own needs, but rather the
needs of others. Since You have been so
gracious to us, help us to forget the sins
that have been committed against us. May
we capture just a bit of Your forgiving
Spirit. In the name of Him who prayed,
"Father forgive them," we also pray. Amen.

God, we know that we can never hide from Your presence. At times this thought is encouraging and at other times it is frightening. Forgive us the times we have vainly tried to hide from You. It was foolish of us to think we could escape Your notice. Just now, instead of hiding, we open our lives to You. We want You to know us and be with us. We repent of our sins in deed and thought. Teach us about ourselves that we might reform our lives in the pattern of Your holiness. May Your Holy Spirit move mightily in our lives. May the people who see us conclude that we have been in Your presence. Instead of keeping You at arm's length, we give ourselves to You wholly. Our lives are now an open book. We are not always proud of what is written there, but we give it to You that You may write a new page. Search us, know us, try us, and lead us. In the name of the One who said, "Lo I am with you always," we pray. Amen.

PASTORAL

Dear God, we thank You that You love us even at our worst. Since You know our every deed and thought, if there were anyone who could rightly reject us it would be You. You did not reject us. You have made us members of the family. You have made us joint-heirs with Christ. You have said You want us to live with You forever. We marvel at this love that sees beyond what we are, and recognizes what we want to be and what we can be. In spite of what we have said and done, and in spite of all the evidence to the contrary, we do want to serve You. Since You know our hearts, You know this is so. We have shown You our worst; help us to display the best, not for our glory, but that the people of this world will give glory to You and to Your dear Son. We pray in His name, amen.

Here we are again, Father, saying the same thing to You. Once again we promise that we will do better. We have said this to You so many times, we are almost embarrassed to say it again. What gives us the courage to keep trying is the reality that we really do want to do better. We don't want to keep making the same mistakes and committing the same sins. We don't want to keep fighting the same bad habits and falling through on our promises. We thank You that You are a God of second chances. More than that, You are a God of third, fourth, and fifth chances. Your grace does not make us arrogant; rather, it fills us with even more resolve to become the kind of Christian who is pleasing to You. We ask not only for forgiveness, but for the encouragement to keep on believing that we will eventually conquer sin in Your name. Through Christ who said, "I have overcome the world," amen.

PASTORAL

This day, dear Father, we would give
thanks for the church. Too often we com-
plain about the church, forgetting that we
are the church. We may have been hurt.
Not every program has filled our needs.
Not every sermon has thrilled our hearts.
Then we stop to think of what we would be
without the church. We think of what worship does to us. We think of the richness
of the fellowship. We think of the love that
has been shared and the times our brothers
and sisters have risen to our aid. We
acknowledge the church as part of Your
plan for us. You knew that we would need
the unique ministry of the local church to
come to full flower in our Christian lives.
Help us to cherish the church. Help us to
serve and support the work of the church.
In the name of Him who called the church
His bride, amen.

Forgive us, our Father, for all the times we thought we could live without You. We were wrapped up in ourselves. We foolishly thought that we could make it on our own. But just when we thought we had everything taken care of, events came into our lives that taught us how much we need You; sickness, family or financial problems, conflict at work or school. Whatever the case, we learned a valuable lesson; we have an incredible need for You. That is something we have in common. We may have different backgrounds and tastes, different habits and hobbies, different talents and temperaments, but we all share a craving for You. We have tried to fill the void with vain pleasures and false masters, but we keep coming back to You. Thank You for accepting prodigals. Thank You for letting us once again wear the robe and the ring. In the name of Jesus, who showed us the way home, we humbly pray. Amen.

PASTORAL

Our Lord, You are God for all ages. When we come to You as children, You comfort us with Your strong hand. When we come to You as confused youth, You forgive and help us through the door to adulthood. As we face the responsibilities of adulthood, You give us courage. When we come to You in later life, You give us strength and reassurance. We do pray for those of our church facing the challenge of each stage of life. Each one has unique joys and challenges. You are our help in ages past. You are our hope for years to come. In the sweet name of our Lord Jesus, amen.

God of power, shock us out of our lethargy. Forgive us when we make Your Word seem dull and Your work a drudgery. You have richly given us all things to enjoy. Forgive us for all the times we looked at the stars and were unimpressed. Forgive us when we faced a waterfall and yawned. Forgive us when we face a new day with dread rather than to see each new day as a gift. We know to reach out to You when life gets hard, but we often forget to reach out to You when life is good. Help us to see that no day is ordinary. Every day is an opportunity for spiritual renewal. Every day is a chance to serve. Every day can become a schoolroom in which we can learn and grow. Help us to treasure our days, and not pass through them half conscious. With our renewed energy we pledge our service, for there are many who need our influence. It is our duty to serve as conduits for Your power. In the name of Jesus, who gave us life abundantly, amen.

PASTORAL

We come to You, our Father, with the delight of children. We ask for Your help because we cannot face our challenges alone. We ask for Your wisdom, since ours is not sufficient for the tasks we face. We ask for Your protection because this world is often dangerous. We ask for our basic needs to be met. We ask most of all for Your presence. As Your children we are delighted to be with You. We know that You will give us exactly what we need. We thank You that You don't always give us what we want. We know You can do anything, and we count on You to do the right thing. Through the Lord Christ, amen.

O God of abundant grace, we come to You as empty vessels waiting to be filled. Sometimes we have been impatient and have filled our lives with things not pleasing to You. Fill us with joy, love, and wisdom. Fill us so full that no impure thought can find a place. Father, we want to be filled to overflowing. We don't need just a little grace, we need a lot of it. With You in our lives we can make changes in ourselves and in this world around us. With Your love in us, we will always have enough love to share with those who are hurting. We will have enough energy to stand up to injustice and to fight suffering. We come to You as beggars. We entreat You as those who hunger and thirst for righteousness. In the name of Jesus, amen.

PASTORAL

Father of light, we ask that You illumine our hearts so that we will shine Your light into a dark world. Forgive us when we have allowed darkness to creep into our souls. Forgive us when we have loved the darkness more than we love the light. May the darkness of sin, fear, and despair be swallowed up in the blazing light of Your loving grace. Give us the resolve to be light-bearers. We pledge ourselves to eliminate the darkness of sin, doubt, unrighteousness, injustice, poverty, and suffering. May the world see Your reflected glory in us. In the name of Jesus, the light of the world, amen.

O God of majesty, You are so mighty
that You are beyond our understanding.
We cannot comprehend Your power. Our
minds cannot conceive of how You spoke
this world into existence. We cannot imagine how You did Your miraculous wonders.
We are especially in awe of the gift of Your
Son. Through Him we can see You and
reach You. Help us to behave in such a
way that the people of this world will see
You in us. Eliminate from our lives any
sin that would mar Your image in us.
Encourage us in our discouragement and
pain so that we can carry on. Strengthen
us as we develop the grace and skill
essential to the mission You have called
us to fulfill. Strengthen us in body and
spirit that we may serve You with enthusiasm. Be with us especially in the time of
discouragement. May Your Spirit be our
comforter, even as You have promised.
Through Your Son, Jesus, amen.

PASTORAL

Mighty and gracious God, we come
before You to today because You have invited us to do so. You are so powerful and
awe-inspiring that we would hardly dare to
approach You if You had not invited us. We
thank You for Your graciousness in time
past. We praise You for the wonders that
draw us to You.

We would also come before You with our
words of confession. We have sinned. We
wish we could say we had not. Some sins
we have committed with forethought.
Some sins we committed by carelessness.
Some are sins of omission. For all of them,
Father, we ask Your mercy. You are a holy
God and we desire to be holy.

We would also place before You our peti-
tions. We ask for stillness for the troubled
heart. We ask for healing and strength to
sick bodies. We ask restoration for broken
relationships. We ask Your blessing upon
Your church. May we never be completely

complacent. We know there are many who still need to hear Your Word. We know there are many who need a word of encouragement. We know there are many who need to be challenged to give of their best to You. Make us the kind of church You are not ashamed to call Your own. Most of all, we thank You for Jesus. His sacrifice is our salvation. His life is our example. As we leave this assembly, may we determine to be like Him and to serve Him. Through Jesus, the great shepherd, we pray. Amen.

PASTORAL

Mighty God, we thank You that though You are the Lord of the universe, You are also the Lord of our hearts. We thank You that You hear us. We implore You to bring peace to our warring world, so that the peoples of the world may live in safety and freedom. We pray especially for those who lack their daily bread. We pray especially for the children, who seem to suffer most. We ask You, Father, to bless our country. Give our leaders wisdom. Help them to see their duties as spiritual service. We beseech You, Lord, for our communities. May we live in harmony and integrity. We beseech You for our church, that we may please You and reflect the beauty of Your Son. We beseech You for our homes. May our families grow in grace and love. We beseech You for ourselves. May we find the power to persevere, and the strength to act justly. In Christ, who revealed to us Your loving heart, we earnestly pray. Amen.

You, our God, are a holy God. We are sinners. We feel humbled in Your presence. Thank You for hearing our cry. Thank You for acting on our behalf. We confess our sins to You, with the confidence that You will destroy the guilt that paralyzes us. You know us very well, dear Father. You know what fills us with fear. You know what tempts us. May Your knowledge of us be turned to benevolent action. We all stand together in desperate need of You. It is not always easy to admit our need, we want so much to be independent. Help us to move from independence to dependence on You. You can make us truly human. You can make us into the image of Your dear Son. In the name of Him who bore our sins and our sorrows, amen.

PASTORAL

You have shown us, O God, Your mighty creativity in nature. How can anyone look to the sky and not think of You? How can anyone walk through a garden and not recognize Your presence? How can people consider the marvel of their own bodies and not give praise to Your name for Your creativity and workmanship? These blessings so often escape our conscious thoughts, but they ought not. If You had done nothing else but give us this wonderful world, that would have been enough to prompt our praise. You have done much more, though. You have given us the blessings of fellowship and forgiveness. You have given us strength for today and hope for tomorrow. We thank You that You have promised us a place even more beautiful than this planet. We look forward to spending forever there with You. May Your Spirit lead us to that end. Through Jesus, the way, the truth, and the life, we pray. Amen.

Help us, our God, to give You our
total attention. All else is confusion and
discord. Help us to examine ourselves in
light of Your revealed Word, for in this
examination we find the secret of new life.
Help us to choose our words carefully, for
with them we can destroy or build up. As
You bless us toward this end, we will give
You our days that we might join with You
in the great enterprise of changing this
world. Through Jesus, who helps us to
see what we can be, amen.

PASTORAL

How much we need You, O God of the brokenhearted. We depend on You for so much. We depend on You for physical and spiritual life. We trust You to be our defender, redeemer, and friend, for without You there is only hopelessness, emptiness, and pain. Mend our broken hearts. Create in us new hearts, if that is what is needed. Help us to rise from our brokenness to sing Your praises, now and forever. Amen.

O God, You are wiser than our understanding and holier than our frail attempts to achieve. You deserve our devotion and praise. You are like the sun You have given us. We see Your warm and constant life-giving energy at work all around us. We see this and think of Your care. We hear the wind You have supplied. It reminds us of Your powerful Holy Spirit, at work changing lives. As we think on these things, our hearts are gladdened even as each new spring gives us hope that death itself must yield to the power of life. In the name of Jesus, whose resurrection gives spring a new and deeper meaning, amen.

PASTORAL

O Lord of grace and glory, we are amazed that You have given us the blessing of pardon. When we think of this blessing, we feel like shouting for joy. Help us to see that grace is for the guilty. We depend on Your understanding, since we have failed You in so many ways at so many times. When we think of this, we are prone to be angry, not at You, but at ourselves. Turn our anger to repentance and our guilt into grace. May Your Spirit help us to rise from our knees with new vigor. In the name of Jesus, who walked this path with us but did not sin, amen.

The heavens declare the glory of God;
the skies proclaim the work of his hands.
Day after day they pour forth speech; night
after night they display knowledge. There
is no speech or language where their voice
is not heard. Their voice goes out into all
the earth, their words to the end of the
world.   Psalm 19:1-4

Remember, O Lord, your great mercy
and love, for they are from of old.

Remember not the sins of my youth and
my rebellious ways; according to your love
remember me, for you are good, O Lord.

Turn to me and be gracious to me, for I
am lonely and afflicted. The troubles of my
heart have multiplied; free me from my
anguish. Look upon my affliction and my
distress and take away all my sins.

Psalm 25:6, 7, 16-18

Blessed is he whose transgressions are forgiven, whose sins are covered. Blessed is the man whose sin the Lord does not count against him and in whose spirit is no deceit.   Psalm 32:1, 2

I will extol the Lord at all times; his praise will always be on my lips. My soul will boast in the Lord; let the afflicted hear and rejoice. Glorify the Lord with me; let us exalt his name together. I sought the Lord, and he answered me; he delivered me from all my fears. Those who look to him are radiant; their faces are never covered with shame. This poor man called and the Lord heard him; he saved him out of all his troubles.   Psalm 34:1-6

Delight yourself in the Lord and he will give You the desires of Your heart. Be still before the Lord and wait patiently for him; do not fret when men succeed in their ways, when they carry out their wicked schemes. Refrain from anger and turn from wrath; do not fret—it leads only to evil. I was young and now I am old, yet I have never seen the righteous forsaken or their children begging bread.

Psalm 37: 4, 7, 8, 25

I waited patiently for the Lord; he turned to me and heard my cry. He lifted out of the slimy pit, out of the mud and mire; he set my feet on a rock and gave me a firm place to stand. He put a new song in my mouth, a hymn of praise to our God. Many will see and fear and put their trust in the Lord.

Psalm 40:1-3

Sing to God, sing praise to his name, extol him who rides on the clouds—his name is the Lord—and rejoice before him. A father to the fatherless, a defender of widows, is God in his holy dwelling. God sets the lonely in families, he leads forth the prisoners with singing; but the rebellious live in a sun-scorched land.

Psalm 68:4-6

When my heart was grieved and my spirit embittered, I was senseless and ignorant; I was a brute beast before you. Yet I am always with you; you hold me by my right hand. You guide me with your counsel, and afterward you will take me into glory. Whom have I in heaven but you? And earth has nothing I desire besides you. My flesh and my heart may fail, but God is the strength of my heart and my portion forever.

Psalm 73:21-26

I cried out to God for help; I cried out to God to hear me. When I was in distress, I sought the Lord; at night I stretched out untiring hands and my soul refused to be comforted. Then I thought, "To this I will appeal: the years of the right hand of the Most High." I will remember the deeds of the Lord; yes, I will remember your miracles of long ago. I will meditate on all your works and consider all your mighty deeds.

Psalm 77:1, 2, 10-12

How lovely is your dwelling place, O Lord Almighty! My soul yearns, even faints, for the courts of the Lord; my heart and my flesh cry out for the living God. Even the sparrow has found a home, and the swallow a nest for herself, where she may have her young—a place near your altar, O Lord Almighty, my King and my God. Blessed are those who dwell in your house; they are ever praising you.

Psalm 84:1-4

Hear, O Lord, and answer me, for I am poor and needy. Guard my life, for I am devoted to You. You are my God; save your servant who trusts in you. Have mercy on me, O Lord, for I call to you all day long. Bring joy to your servant, for to you, O Lord, I lift up my soul. You are forgiving and good, O Lord, abounding in love to all who call to you. Hear my prayer, O Lord; listen to my cry for mercy. In the day of my trouble I will call to you, for you will answer me.   Psalm 86:1-7

Praise the Lord, O my soul; all my inmost being, praise his holy name. Praise the Lord, O my soul, and forget not all his benefits–who forgives all your sins and heals all your diseases, who redeems your life from the pit and crowns you with love and compassion, who satisfies your desires with good things so that your youth is renewed like the eagle's. The Lord is compassionate and gracious, slow to anger, abounding in love. He will not always accuse, nor will he harbor his anger forever; he does not treat us as our sins deserve or repay us according to our iniquities. For as high as the heavens are above the earth, so great is his love for those who fear him; as far as the east is from the west, so far has he removed our transgressions from us.

Psalm 103:1-5, 8-12

Give thanks to the Lord, call on his name; make known among the nations what he has done. Sing to him, sing praise to him; tell of all his wonderful acts. Glory in his holy name; let the hearts of those who seek the Lord rejoice.

Psalm 105:1-3

Open my eyes that I may see wonderful things in your law. Turn my eyes away from worthless things; preserve my life according to your word. I will never forget your precepts, for by them you have preserved my life. How sweet are your words to my taste, sweeter than honey to my mouth! Great peace have they who love your law, and nothing can make them stumble.

Psalm 119:18, 37, 93, 103, 165

My heart is not proud, O Lord, my eyes are not haughty; I do not concern myself with great matters or things too wonderful for me. But I have stilled and quieted my soul; like a weaned child with its mother, like a weaned child is my soul within me.

Psalm 131:1, 2

NEW YEAR

O God, as we look into a new year, we are filled with regrets, fear, and hope. Regrets that we did not fulfill our resolutions last year, fear that we will fail again, and hope that You will forgive our failures and empower us for new victories. We thank You that You are more than a God of second chances, for we need many more chances than that. We acknowledge this new year as a fresh opportunity. No doubt we will sometimes fail, but may we find in this new year that we will grow in knowledge, discipline, righteousness, and love. God, we thank You that You are indeed "our help in ages past, our hope for years to come." In the name of Him who said, "I make all things new," our Lord Jesus Christ, we pray. Amen.

Dear Father, young people are special gifts, and we ask You to make us aware of our responsibilities toward them. We often call them the church of tomorrow, but help us to recognize they are part of the church of today. May we honor the contributions they make even now. We thank You for their energy and enthusiasm. We thank You for their inquisitive minds. We thank You that they love You. Help us not to condemn but to compliment. Help us to give them roots and wings. In the name of Jesus, who always had time for the young, amen.

GOOD FRIDAY

O Lord of salvation, we remember Your mighty work of redemption accomplished on the cross. We can see the rough-hewn wood. We can see the Lord Jesus burdened as He walked the dusty roads to the place of the skull. We can hear the jeers, the crying, the hammer blows. When we think of these things, we are filled with both sorrow and joy—sorrow, that our sins put Jesus there, but also joy for what He accomplished on that cross. Help us to see that at Calvary, a place of death, Jesus gave us life. Bring these scenes before us, if we ever forget the beauty of the sacrifice. Through Christ, who bore our sins in His body on the tree, amen.

Lord God Almighty, we celebrate this day as the focal point of history as well as the focal point of our lives. We thank You for the testimony of the empty tomb. More than that, we thank You for the testimony of a world filled with the presence of the risen Lord. We praise Your holy name that love wins out over hate, hope wins out over despair, faith wins out over doubt, and life wins out over death. We acknowledge that without the resurrection our lives would be futile. The resurrection is the most astounding fact in this world, a one-time event worthy of our celebration. In Christ our hope we pray, amen.

EASTER

God of life, we give You praise for the promise of resurrection. Every spring we see how You have written *resurrection* into nature itself. Every Sunday, as we gather in the community of believers, we see how You have written *resurrection* into history. Every time we stand before a grave and feel the longings for life eternal, we see how You have written *resurrection* into our hearts. This takes away the fear and dread of the tomb. No longer can we see death the same way. While it is still mysterious and somewhat frightening, we know that it is a defeated enemy. If the worst that death can do to us is to usher us into Your presence, it cannot do us harm. We thank You that Jesus won the victory. We thank You that He holds the key to life eternal and that He has led the way. May we live our lives with the kind of optimism that the resurrection brings. In the name of the risen One, amen.

EASTER

Father of victory, this is the day when words fail us. This is the day when we ponder the most dramatic event in the history of this world. This is the day when we celebrate the fact that You brought Jesus out of the grave. Our minds can barely hold that thought, yet we are captivated by it.

We celebrate Your victory over the treacheries and tragedies of this world. We celebrate Your victory over hatred and cynicism. We celebrate Your victory over death itself.

We thank You not only for the empty grave, but also for the presence of the risen Lord who is still conquering today. We thank You that His resurrection makes possible our own. We pray that the resurrection power will be evident in our lives.

Forgive us for living on the wrong side of Easter, as if Jesus were still in the grave. May our full hearts be a testimony of the empty tomb. Through Jesus who lives, amen.

MOTHER'S DAY

Dear Lord of the family, on this day
we give You thanks for our mothers. We
honor those who bore us, nurtured us,
protected us, and supported us. Although
we can never fully know how important
their service was, we know our lives would
be poverty-stricken without them. We
remember the mothers who have gone to
glory and we honor them. We give thanks
and pledge our support for the mothers
still among us. We pray for special
strength for those currently engaged in
the difficult task of parenting. If our
relationship with our mother is troubled,
we pray, dear God, for forgiveness and
reconciliation. Father, we pray for those
who desire to be mothers, but have not yet
conceived. We pray that You will answer
their longings, either through a birth or by
bringing them a precious soul who needs
their mothering care. Through Jesus, who
longed to gather us together as a mother
hen gathers her chicks, amen.

Help us, mighty God, never to take lightly the sacrifices people have made of Your most precious gift of life. We know that those who gave their lives did not do so lightly, but they did so willingly. We are the benefactors of their sacrifice. Help us to honor them by always remembering. Help us to honor them by giving something back to our world, nation, and community. We will remember and be encouraged by the great cloud of witnesses. Through Jesus who gave His life for even His enemies, amen.

PENTECOST

You are holy, God, and You know us well. You know our need for companionship. You know our need for corporate worship. For this reason, You gave us the church. On this anniversary of the birthday of the church, we recall the powerful manifestation of Your Spirit. We pray that Your Spirit might move among us in a similar way today. We owe so much to the church, more than we can ever fully realize. While Your church is filled with imperfect people, it still reaches out and changes the world through the preaching of the gospel. In the name of Christ, the head of the church, amen.

We give You praise, dear Father of all wisdom, for the gift of knowledge. We honor today those who have persevered in the pursuit of academic achievement. We trust that You will help them to know not just facts, but to know You. Help each graduate to add to their knowledge the wisdom essential for the application of knowledge to the achievement of godly aims. Help these graduates use the resources they have been given to improve society, the home, and the church. We desire to love You with heart, soul, mind, and strength. Through Jesus, our great teacher, amen.

FATHER'S DAY

Dear God, we marvel that You have exalted fatherhood by asking us to call You *Father*. On this day, help us to remember and appreciate the impact our fathers have made on our lives.

We pledge ourselves to respect those of our fathers who are still with us on this earth. We pledge ourselves to honor the memories of those fathers who have left this life to stand before You.

God, we ask that You will help those whose relationships with their fathers is difficult or even tragic. We ask for comfort and we ask for forgiveness.

Those of us who are fathers ask You for wisdom and strength to be the kind of fathers our children need and deserve.

We pray especially that all fathers will give glory to You.

Through Jesus, who taught us to call You *Father,* amen.

Lord, keep us from the foolishness of thinking that You love Americans more than Your saints in other lands. Give us the wisdom to recognize and thank You for the many blessings You have given us in this free nation. Help us to remember that to whom much is given, much is expected. Help us as a nation to reflect Your truth. It is our prayer that You will mend every flaw. Help us to be a land whose God is the Lord. Through Christ, in whom there is no east or west, amen.

THANKSGIVING

We are prone, our God, to think only of the material things this season. While we do appreciate the things You have given us to enjoy—life, food, good health, family, and friends—we know there are more important things. We would be remiss indeed if we limited our thanks to the obvious. We thank You for giving us hope. We thank You for giving us forgiveness. We thank You for giving us yourself. We are so grateful for these things that the word *thanks* is too small. In Christ our life, we pray, amen.

Dear God, we should thank You every day, but we do not. We experience countless blessings and walk past them as if they were not there. We receive so much from You each day that we could never thank You enough. Still, we want to give special attention to our thanks on this special day. Even in the worst of times, we have much to be grateful for. Give us an attitude of gratitude. Move us beyond a complaining and critical spirit. Help us look past our struggles and trials to see that we have a relationship with You that should prompt the highest thanks. If You were all we had, You would be enough. We remember, dear Father, how our Lord Jesus gave thanks even on the night He was betrayed. May we live with that kind of insight and sensitivity. In His glorious name we pray, amen.

THANKSGIVING

God, there is so much to thank You for and so little time. Not only will we run out of time, we will also run out of words. So often we tend to blame You for every bad thing, but fail to thank You for every good thing. We confess that we do not deserve the blessings we have, yet we have confidence that even more will come. We thank You for the ultimate blessing: the promise of Your presence. If that's all we had, we would still need to say *thank You*. The saints of old gave thanks to You and they had much less than we. We are often unable to recognize how blessed we are. We are often ashamed of our lack of appreciation. Keep us ever mindful of those who are less fortunate. Help us to do Your work so that they may enjoy the blessing that can come to all. Through Jesus, life's greatest blessing, amen.

Father of light, although this world is exceedingly dark, it does serve as a contrast that Your star may been seen more brightly. Never has the world needed Your light more. Every corner of this planet has been corrupted by wickedness. Our own hearts have been compromised. May Your Christmas light point the world back to the Christ. Help us to minister to the destitute in our nation and in nations around the world. Help us to minister to them in a way that beings glory to You and makes them open to the good news of Jesus Christ. Help us to honor the poor, since Your Son was born among the poorest of the poor. In the name of Him who had no place to lay His head, amen.

CHRISTMAS

Father of all joy, take us once again to Bethlehem. Help us to experience the excitement of the shepherds in ancient times who first heard the good news of great joy. Give us the same sense of wonder that they had long ago. Help us to feel the surprise. Let this familiar story warm our hearts. Help us, like them, to waste no time in finding the Lord Jesus. Help us, like them, to tell everyone we see about Him. May the good news that started around the world that day be ever in our minds and hearts. May His name be ever on our lips. As the news that night changed the lives of humble shepherds, may it change our lives today, for we are in need of good news. Real Christmas joy will change our homes, our lives, and our world. O holy child of Bethlehem, be born in us today. May our hearts be like that manger of old that accepted the Christ. May we make room for Him in our lives, in whose name we pray. Amen.

Father, in this season it is sometimes hard to hear You amid the sound of cash registers and beeping toys. It is hard to see You beyond the garish light of holiday displays. This season, above all, we should seek Your face. If we miss You, we have surely missed it all. In spite of all noise, we attune our ears to You. Help us hear the sounds of the angel chorus. Help us see the light of the ancient star. Above all, let us hear the baby's cry, a cry that tells us You are among us to seek and to save that which is lost. We pray in the name of Jesus, the baby in the manger and the man on the cross, amen.

CHRISTMAS

May the joy of the season draw us to the Christ even as the ancient star led wise men of old to His side. Let our curiosity prompt us to make the pilgrimage in our minds and in our hearts. Let us see that the trip is worth it all. How tragic it would be if we celebrated without a reason or for the wrong reason. How sad if we were to forget whose birthday it is. Though the rest of the world may make merry without any real understanding, we will celebrate Your Son. Through Christ, the reason for it all, amen.

Holy God, You are powerful, yet compassionate. We plead with You to act with mercy. We confess that at times we do not understand, particularly when bad things happen to good people. Our hearts are heavy under this terrible burden. We see the look of despair. We see the tears of the hurting. When we see these things we are troubled, because something tells us it should be better than this. Help us to remember that the something that tells us there is something better is really a person. It is You. Although You did not promise that life on this earth would be without pain, You will balance all the scales in eternity. Help us also to remember that when we face suffering here, You are with us and we can feel Your hand. Help us to make this earth more like Heaven if we can, but never let us forget that the glory of Heaven is Your ultimate goal for us. Through Jesus, who suffered even though He was perfect, amen.

A TIME OF TRAGEDY

Be with us, Father, in the midst of our pain. It is in times such as these that You seem far away. Even when You seem farther away than the most distant star, help us to feel Your hand on our shoulder. Help us to understand that You hurt when we hurt and weep when we weep. Help us to see that there is no time You are nearer than when we are in pain. We thank You, Father, that we can feel pain. If we felt no pain, we could feel no joy either. We give all our feelings to You. Bottle our tears as precious ointment, and send us relief. We pray in Jesus' name, amen.